Praise for *On Recruitment*

"The recruitment world is a noisy world and cutting through all the bluster is Mitch Sullivan. If you have anything whatsoever to do with the job hunting or recruitment, then I highly recommend reading this book. It's intelligent, well-written, funny and thought provoking with the added benefit of Mitch not being scared to say what needs to be said. Whether you like it or not."

Jonathan Reed, Conrad Brookes R2R

"Mitch is a writer you are compelled to read. Just not aloud and when children are present."

Steve Ward, Social Media Recruitment Expert

"Mitch is a recruiter with over 25 years industry experience who writes about whatever the hell he likes. He is massively opinionated but often hits the nail on the head. On a personal level I've known Mitch for 20 years and during that time have often wanted to punch him in the face. I've just as often laughed out loud at his superb sense of humour and writing style."

Louise Triance, Founder, ukrecruiter.co.uk

"This is a book of home truths for those who are not easily offended. Grab a beer, and argue with the author from first to last page."

Bill Boorman, Founder, Tru Conferences

D0957810

"Mitch is capable of picking intellectual holes in hot fashions and hyped-up trends, showing how they are often little more than fluff and fairy tales. He'll then jolt you back into the real world with his energetic form of cynicism that draws on established truths and a creative examination of future possibilities."

Dr Richard Claydon, Management Consultant

"They say written content can't carry tone. They also say recruiters are all the same and just worried about their next fee. Mitch Sullivan proves both statements wrong. You can hear his dulcet, witty tones in everything he writes. He's renowned as one of the voices of our industry."

Tom Wish, Content Manager, Hunted

"If run-of-the-mill, emotionless recruitment fare is your thing, don't bother reading this book. Mitch has a reputation for beautifully dissecting an industry so often bound by bullshit. Strap yourself in, folks!"

Simon Lewis, MD, onlymarketingjobs.com

About Mitch Sullivan

Mitch started out in recruitment 29 years ago.

He did the normal contingency agency role as Consultant, Manager then Troubleshooter (although not in that order) for a couple of the large national UK sales recruitment specialists before moving to Geneva, Switzerland.

There he set up a different kind of search and selection business – one that focused on using creative recruitment communications as its primary source of recruiting local talent for the large local multinational businesses and which combined hard-nosed commercial consultancy with innovative recruitment marketing. That creative approach to recruitment advertising proved popular and further innovation followed in the shape of the region's first ever online candidate database web portal called virtualjobagency.com.

On returning to the UK in 2005, he broadened his appreciation of corporate recruiting by working as an Interim Recruitment Manager for a number of large UK corporates, helping them to develop their direct sourcing and employment branding capabilities and filling jobs they and their external agency partners were struggling with.

Today he plies his trade as a recruiter (servicing the SME sector) and coaching recruiters. His website can be found at www.fasttrackrecruitment.com.

ON RECRUITMENT

Carefully treading the fine line between
cynicism and evangelism

Mitch Sullivan

ISBN 978-1-9999293-0-5

Contents

PART 3 – Recruitment Agencies

Introduction

This book is a collection of 44 of the 150 or so blogs I've written over recent years. They are all about the world of hiring people to do jobs in exchange for money – or to give it its snappier title; recruitment – a profession I've given nearly 30 years of my life to. It has been a love/hate kind of relationship – something that will probably become evident during your reading of this book.

The book is divided into three parts. The first part contains blogs about the broader context of the world of recruitment, hiring and job-seeking. The second has blogs that focus more on hiring companies and inhouse recruiters and the third predominantly looks at issues that relate more to the 3rd party agency sector.

Even though I've also worked inhouse and produced hundreds of recruitment marketing campaigns, I'm essentially an agency guy at heart – and it's that perspective that influences much of my view of the industry.

This book is dedicated to all the people who, over the past 15 years, have listened to my arguments and opinions on recruitment and who have disagreed with me and tried to show me why I'm wrong. Some of them know who they are.

What I'm really saying here is that these blogs have been researched and tested in the white-hot forum of online debate and any number of inner-city pubs and bars.

These blogs have made me some friends as well as some enemies over the past few years.

If after reading this book you fall into the 2nd category, there will be no refunds.

PART 1

The Recruitment Market

1. Bad news

The most common gripe candidates have with recruiters is that they don't get back to them.

Generally, that means either being called by a recruiter about a potential new role and then hearing nothing, not getting any kind of response to a job application or not getting feedback after an interview.

But, in my experience, the single most common way a candidate lets a recruiter know that they're not interested in a previously discussed job, is to not return phone calls or emails.

Which is ironic.

This isn't an excuse to not give feedback to candidates. I'm just saying that it's not a behavioural trait that's exclusive to recruiters, that's all.

I think we all should just accept that most people don't like delivering bad news and will avoid it wherever possible.

If you're one of those recruiters that can and does deliver bad news with a degree of compassion and honesty, you'll be remembered as one of those "good recruiters".

Being good at it is a way of standing out from the crowd – especially if these are people you may want to talk to again.

People can be unreliable.

Welcome to recruitment.

2. Do passive candidates read job adverts?

Before writing this blog, I went to LinkedIn and crowd-sourced the opinions of anyone who cared to express one.

I was surprised by the results. I was expecting more recruiters to say that the only way to find passive candidates was to source them directly. Maybe they were pandering to me in the knowledge that I am something of an evangelist when it comes to producing good job copy.

I was especially encouraged by the comments posted by non-recruiters (also sometimes known as candidates and clients), many of whom suggested that for them to respond whilst browsing job ads at a time when they didn't actually *need* another job, the ad would need to stand out from the others and/or be remarkable in some way.

What that means in basic terms is looking at a page of search results for, let's say a Marketing Manager, and not seeing opening sentences in each advert summary like:

"We need..."

"We are seeking..."

"You will be responsible for..."

Instead of something that potentially relates to their needs or intrigues them, like:

"Still not got that promotion you've been hoping for?"

"Here's proof you're not earning what you're worth."

"My English teacher used to tell me to avoid the word 'nice'..."

Opening sentences like those last three are called *attention grabbers* or *pattern disruptors*.

They're designed to encourage people to click and to read further and they work – but only if the job advert then lives up to the inherent promise made in that opening line.

There's a standard sales tactic that many agency recruiters use in conversations with hiring authorities. It's one that evolved in the early 2000s when the Internet, LinkedIn and Job Boards had started to democratise the sourcing of potential candidates.

It goes something like this: "The best candidates aren't browsing job ads because they're too busy being good at their current job. We specialise in finding candidates who are in the market, not on the market."

This particular piece of sales rhetoric became especially popular around 15 or so years ago when many recruitment agencies stopped being horizontal market specialists and started being vertical market specialists. It's where the 24-year-old International Headhunter (who a year ago was selling mobile phones in your local high street) was first born.

The problem is of course that they're not really Headhunters and they don't know how to attract people to jobs who are otherwise reasonably happy where they are.

The flood of automated agency emails containing awful job content is testimony to that.

The reality is that so-called "passive candidates" are far more likely to respond to an advert, a social media update, an email or a phone call if the job in question potentially offers them something their current job doesn't offer. And that something is almost never a bigger salary cheque.

However, the logic of my argument notwithstanding, this is just anecdotal evidence from a handful of comments on LinkedIn and a recruiter with copywriting courses to sell.

Empirical data on recruitment activity is, and always has been, difficult to come by.

This is largely because those who have the most of it (recruitment agencies) either don't want to share it or don't measure very much of it, so I'll end this blog with an attempt to offer more scientific clues that strongly suggest passive candidates do look at job ads.

A quick perusal of Google Trends shows that as many people are searching for jobs as they were back in the recession years of 2008 to 2010. Depending on the job discipline, sometimes it's more.

So firstly, people in general are still typing some kind of job related search term into Google.

They're looking, but are they reacting?

Secondly, according to some of the analysis from reputable recruitment service providers like Social Talent and Jobvite, the percentage of job ad viewers who do not click "apply" is around 98%.

Think about that one for a moment.

For every hundred people who go to the effort of searching for the term "marketing jobs", only 2 are responding to those jobs they see advertised.

Thirdly, Clinch, a recruitment marketing and CRM platform, suggests that according to their data, the majority of viewers of job ads are passive. I quote: "The research showed that a large proportion of people who look at jobs are primarily looking for new opportunities, they already have a job but are looking to improve their situation. Better salary, better conditions, promotion opportunities, the reasons are many and varied."

Bottom line?

Potential candidates are looking in the shop window but not walking into the shop.

So, to answer the question posed in the headline; yes, passive candidates *do* read job adverts if they're worth reading.

And if they like what they read, some of them will get in touch.

Those that don't get in touch, might just remember you when they are ready.

But they'll only remember you if your ads don't read like all the others.

3. Stupid candidates

Do you want to get a lot fewer unsuitable job applications?

Of course you do. What are you, a masochist?

Here's what you need to do.

Make your job ads shorter. Much shorter.

150 words is easier (not to mention more inviting) to read than six hundred and seventy-eight words. As is 150 when written numerically.

Plus, there's the Internet, which has apparently reduced our attention spans.

Most Landscape Gardeners don't really want to be a Project Manager for an IT company – especially once they know what's involved.

But they see an ad for a Project Manager and might have a thought process that looks something like: "Hey, I manage garden projects and can sort stuff out. Plus the money's great…"

Then they look at the length of the ad and the density of the text and think "Screw that, I'll just send my CV anyway. You never know. Plus, they're an agency so they might have something else..."

OK, you may argue that anyone who thinks like that is stupid. I would argue that they're more likely to just be desperate for another job.

Them being desperate could be because there's a declining need for people with their skills or it could be because they're trying to escape long-term unemployment or English isn't their first language.

Being desperate doesn't make someone stupid.

If you *make them* read your ad? If you have an easy-to-read piece of content that is clear on what it's asking for, then most of those Landscape Gardeners won't apply.

Why would they?

Most of them aren't stupid and even more of them don't want to appear stupid to anyone else – even if that someone else is an anonymous remote person they'll never meet.

That's why, when you invite people to phone rather than send a CV, you magically don't get calls from the wildly inappropriate. That's because they know they're not right and don't want the humiliation of trying to explain themselves to someone on the other end of a phone.

Because that's how people are. It's a human-nature thing.

Now, if one of them reads the shorter ad and still applies, chances are they're a moron.

Those I can't help you with.

Don't post job descriptions and expect them to behave like job advertisements.

And stop posting stupid job ads if you don't want stupid applications from candidates who probably aren't stupid.

4. Let's change recruitment forever!

Everyone seems to want to "reinvent" recruitment.

Or "disrupt" it.

Or, in the case of some of the clowns out there, "change it forever".

Apparently, the latest big idea is that a company that will remain nameless (because they're idiots) are going to "change recruitment forever" by introducing some digital tech that will make it easy for everyone in the company to be a recruiter by referring their friends for jobs.

Yeah, I know. Genius.

Corporate employee referral programmes already don't work in sufficient numbers to be all the evidence needed to know that people won't start recommending other people they know to work at their company unless it somehow connects to their own self-interests.

Plus, when you start successfully filling a place of work with staff who are friends, family or acquaintances then the gene pool is already nearing the line in the sand that says "retardation".

The thing that all the recruitment gurus and disruptors refuse to acknowledge is that recruitment is what it is because of people – and unless someone comes up with a piece of tech that removes the human element altogether –

only then can I see it becoming remotely predictable.

But.

There is a piece of old tech out there that could change recruitment.

Last year the *Washington Post* published a blog that suggests there is no evidence that interviewing job applicants prompts better hiring decisions.

My own 143 years of experience in the recruitment industry (that's dog years by the way) has brought me to a place where I find myself agreeing with this premise.

I've seen too many candidates who have almost totally matched the brief I've been working to, not get the job.

Sometimes I've even squirmed with embarrassment for the line manager when listening to their attempted rationale for hiring someone, when what they really wanted to say was "I've just got a hunch about this one".

So, what can we do about candidate selection to make it fairer for everybody involved?

This is a tough one and I'm sure it's a question that the Recruitment Futurologists (the planet's true failed recruiters) will dissect to death over the coming months, years, decades, millennia.

Putting on my borrowed recruitment futurology hat, I pondered this same question for what felt like a lifetime, but was in fact only 7½ minutes.

You put all the shortlisted candidate names into a hat (or a big drum if it's a big shortlist) and basically do a prize draw.

First name drawn gets the job.

Second name gets the job in case the other person turns it down.

And the third name gets a department store voucher for 25 quid.

You could turn it into a bit of an event. Get a few beers in, some nibbles and maybe YouTube it as the theme for a new employer branding video.

What difference would it make to British industry if companies selected candidates this way?

Would work performance really suffer some seismic shift downwards?

Think of all the management time that could be saved not having to interview people, not to mention the reduction in stress.

No doubt some Big Data Scientist will come along soon and tell me that not interviewing people really is going to become the future. No wait, that's what the Futurologists do, right?

Seriously, run with the Tombola idea for a while.

5. Fuck the recruitment industry

This is the sentiment that pretty much sums up the current state of my industry if my LinkedIn feed is anything to go by.

People, it seems, are not happy with recruitment agencies.

People (who sometimes also go by the name of "candidates") are complaining that they don't get phone calls returned.

Companies are moaning about being sent speculative anonymous CVs.

And IT people are doing what they always do – crying like babies every time they get an email telling them about a job they're not interested in.

Maybe it's just a blip; corporate UK having a temporary hormonal crisis.

Or maybe me seeing a lot of these negative posts right now is just a coincidence.

I don't know.

But I am a little surprised.

I thought the Internet had been around long enough for everyone to have read enough about other people's experiences with recruitment suppliers to have worked it all out by now.

That recruitment is a shitty business.

But it seems they haven't.

Today, the dynamic between agencies and hiring companies (sometimes also known as "clients") seems even more Sisyphean than it's ever been.

Even though candidate data is widely available to anyone who can be bothered to go look for it, recruitment agencies are still trying to do business on contingency and wondering why they keep getting shafted – either by the hiring company, the candidate or another agency.

And that probably just makes many of them behave even worse. Like fat kids who keep hearing the word "no".

The more well-meaning agency recruiters will respond to these criticisms of their industry by saying "we're not all like that" and other similarly bimboesque bullshit.

Often, they're active members of a recruitment trade body like the REC – an organisation seemingly intent on preserving its Munchausen Syndrome by Proxy relationship with a recruitment industry that, if it were a person, would have been certified as brain-damaged by now.

I know there's a minority of recruiters trying to do things differently – and that is encouraging – but in the big scheme of things, as an industry we're still frogs that haven't worked out we're in a saucepan, let alone realising that the water is gradually getting hotter.

I've even had some of my peers tell me that, because I have a large network/following of recruiters, I should be more responsible in what I say about my sector.

That I shouldn't agree with these complaints from, what are, in essence, our customers.

That I should defend the industry.

Really?

If you care that much, build your own network of recruiters and preach your apologist bullshit to them yourself.

Before you start kicking me in the nuts by accusing me of just being a cynical has-been, as an external recruitment supplier, I'm still filling jobs at a 90% success rate. Which means I'm comfortable with my minuscule contribution to the recruitment gene pool. I'm not pissing off any candidates or pebble-dashing hiring manager's inboxes with anonymous CVs and labelling them as "top talent" who "really want to work for your company".

Hell, I even offer to train recruiters for less money than falls out of James Caan's pockets in loose change every month.

So fuck it. I'm trying, OK?

If I sometimes take the piss out of the industry, it's because it's begging to have the piss taken out of it. Just like all those silly fuckers that have ever appeared on *The Apprentice*.

I wish I had all the answers to this malaise, but I don't.

But what I do know is that companies get the agency representation they deserve.

Because if a company is too lazy to do some basic due-diligence on a recruitment agency before engaging with them, they deserve everything they get.

It takes about 10 minutes to get a snapshot of an agency's DNA just by looking at the number of clichés they use on their website, the background and average length of stay of their staff and the quality of their jobs advertising.

And another 10 minutes to instruct them on precisely how they want them to behave. Just like they presumably do with all the other external suppliers they use?

But instead, they dish out jobs like confetti to anyone with less than 3-years total work experience and who are now branding themselves as a "Talent Acquisition Consultant" who 6 months ago were working as a sales assistant in River Island. Talent Acquisition Consultants whose only way of determining talent is by counting the number of matching keywords on the job specification and the CV.

Some companies get away with it because they've got names like Barclays or Vodafone. And because the agencies don't tell the target candidates who they're trying to fill these jobs for, until the more desperate of those candidates have responded positively to their typo-strewn emails.

So much for talent acquisition.

Agencies keep doing it because they do enough numbers to sometimes draw out responses from those who need another job/contract. In short, it works. The collateral damage is high, but when it comes to making money, who gives a shit?

Eventually, everyone forgets the names of the agencies that pissed them off. Then the whole cyclical clusterfuck starts up all over again a few weeks later.

So, if you're a hiring company and aren't smart enough to see this and to do something about it, fuck you.

And if you're an agency recruiter who thinks it's best to blindly defend the industry, fuck you too.

6. Who cares about candidates?

I think the formalisation of the concept of "Candidate Experience" is now just another of those "emperor's new clothes" things that pop up from time to time.

It's something I used to think made sense for hiring companies and recruiters to care about – and at its rudimentary level it still does make sense.

The problem is, now it's been hijacked by marketers keen to find a new garden to piss in.

The only people with the inclination and the money to buy into "candidate experience" as a new part of the recruiting process to obsess about are, ironically, the very people who don't need it.

Namely, large corporates with omnipresent brands who are not going to lose any consumers who have temporarily doubled up as a candidate just because they didn't get a response to their job application.

Of course there's always an exception, like everyone's favourite cable company Virgin Media, who re-examined their application process in order to save around £4 million. There's nothing like a big pile of cash to encourage people to do the right thing.

But for almost every other large corporate, their recruitment process screams out "Hey, we're doing you a favour just by having job vacancies you ungrateful drones".

It's the same dynamic at play where people allow themselves to be treated like shit by those that are rich and powerful. But when someone from their own peer group does it, out comes the righteous indignation.

There is a school of thought that for a company to build a great candidate experience requires great recruiters – something I kind of agree with.

The problem is, they don't pay internal recruiters anywhere near enough to attract the best.

And they probably don't need to either.

I think the reality is that large corporates are only an option for 3 types of recruiters:

1. Ambitious recruiters who want to learn more about the recruitment landscape so they can take that learning back to agency-land a year or two later and make some real money putting it into practice.

2. Older agency recruiters who have finally been beaten down by the bullshit that is contingency recruitment.

3. HR people who are into masochism.

The fact that corporate recruiters need to bother themselves with candidate experience issues is just one of the prices they have to pay for working there.

That and the institutional arrogance their employer has when it comes to hiring. The main reason I stopped working with large corporates about 5 years ago, was this attitude that they didn't need to put any effort into attracting new hires.

Life's too short to work alongside that kind of arrogance every day. Well, at least my life is.

Apart from large corporates, nobody cares about "the candidate experience". And they only care about it as another branding bauble to hoodwink the world with.

Even candidates don't care about it.

If companies really cared about what candidates experienced when applying for their jobs, they'd be more careful about which recruitment agencies they use.

The day "candidate experience" became a thing, was also the day it started being bullshit.

Since when did treating candidates with basic courtesy ever need to have its own chapter in the recruiting "How to" guide?

7. What is the real problem with recruitment?

It would seem recruiters are disliked. Even internal recruiters.

How much they're disliked will probably depend on the part of the market they work.

For example, IT recruiters are far more disliked than executive search consultants. The latter go into things in a lot more detail and tend to be more commercially mature, whereas too many of the former are just spot-traders of CVs and keywords.

How much recruiters are disliked will also depend on the level of client and/or candidate expectation.

Sales recruiters will have greater expectation put on them than the generalist/high street operators. The generalists are expected to be little more than enthusiastic administrators, whilst the sales recruiters are expected to know how to sell so they can spot others who know how to sell.

But why are they disliked?

I don't think it can't just be explained away as it being an industry with a low barrier to entry and therefore overly populated with people who are still at that stage where they don't really know what they're doing. Like dogs that still chase cars.

In almost any other job discipline, not really knowing what you're doing tends to be quite self-evident. A marketer who doesn't know much about marketing is quite easy to spot within a few minutes of conversation.

If the online commentary from hiring managers and candidates is to be believed, the bad recruiters aren't being spotted because they're still regularly getting plenty of opportunities to charge fees for candidates that often don't turn out to be "top talent" like the brochure promised.

So let's take a step back for a moment and broaden the view of the recruitment landscape.

The Internet and social media is full of service providers claiming to reinvent, revolutionise or disrupt the recruitment industry.

Services from flat-fee recruiters promising great returns from posting boring job ads on lots of different job boards, to software vendors claiming their technology will make managing candidates and filling jobs easier.

There are online portals that try to price-fix and manage the relationship between the agency and the client – like that particular dynamic ever needed to be made more remote.

Then there are the recruitment trainers who promise to make agency recruiters temporarily better at offering a service called contingency that most companies don't really need.

Lots of easy button solutions to complicated problems.

But wait, there's more.

Recruitment extends far beyond recruitment agencies and recruitment-related vendors.

There are recruitment Preferred Supplier Lists being managed by HR and procurement administrators.

CEOs who proclaim, "people are our greatest asset", yet pay scant attention to how their business attracts and assesses future employees.

Hiring managers who don't want to interview people.

HR people who don't know how to assess potential recruitment suppliers and who listen to an agency recruiter say, "We're experts in your field" with a sense of relief rather than a sense of suspicion.

Marketing departments that produce job ads that only talk about themselves and what they want, instead of trying to address the needs of the reader.

In essence, what we have are hiring companies who act like they're doing the world a favour just by having job vacancies.

Then there are the candidates, who probably know less about recruitment than anyone and who often act like they're the most qualified applicant out of 200.

What we're left with is a recruitment Wild West where half the community are scrambling for the "gold in them hills" they've been lied to about with the other half trying to sell them everything from shovels to mining equipment.

No one gets out of this entirely blameless. And almost everyone seems to be trying to pass the buck.

Candidates lie to agencies and interviewers about their work experience and why they're on the market.

Agencies lie to hiring managers and HR about what they can and can't deliver.

HR lie to agencies and their own senior management teams about why they can't fill jobs.

And worst of all, CEOs, MDs, hiring managers and agency recruiters all lie to themselves.

But it all boils down to one thing.

The work.

When it comes to hiring, very few of those with a stake in the outcome seem to want to do any.

Filling jobs is hard work.

Part of what makes it hard is that it's work that involves dealing with people who, for the most part, don't want to be there. And of all the people involved in a recruitment process, those that want to be there the least are the candidates.

People dislike doing recruitment because recruitment can be, and often is, a shitty job.

It's a job that tries to fill a rational process with irrational participants. A bit like trying to hold a debate about humanitarianism with only *Daily Mail* readers on the panel.

Recruitment, when done poorly, is a shitty job because it involves cold-calling, taking a poor brief, looking at thousands of CVs, getting rejected by qualified candidates and being pursued by those that aren't, never really knowing where the next fee is coming from and only ever getting paid for 20% of all their activity. Welcome to the world of recruitment agencies and RPOs.

Recruitment, when done properly, is still a shitty job because it requires the person to first own the vacancy they're trying to fill – and then to be good at research, sales, marketing, assessment, management and admin. There isn't a person alive anywhere who's good at all those things.

Recruitment has lots of moving parts and enough that can go wrong to sometimes make a fool of even the very best practitioners.

It's a job that no one else really wants to do – no one outside of the recruitment industry that is. And they mainly do it because they're able to charge a lot of money for it.

Whether that "it" is a comprehensive search and selection process or simply the touting of a candidate with all the right keywords, what makes the shittiness bearable is that it can be financially rewarding.

So, all you HR people, hiring managers, CEOs and business owners, if you don't like the way agencies earn their money, fill your own jobs.

If your internal recruitment staff aren't filling enough jobs themselves, fire them, employ better recruiters and pay them more.

If you want to know if a candidate is one of the best currently available, interview more than 2 people.

If you want agencies to earn their money, make them earn it. Here's how you make an agency earn their fee:

1. Pick one agency after having assessed them thoroughly.

2. Brief them properly and tell them the truth.

3. Give them what they need to do the job properly. Put yourself in their shoes.

4. Have them work to a pre-agreed assignment plan.

If you don't know how to select and manage recruitment agencies properly, find someone who does.

Recruiters earn more money than you think they deserve because they're prepared to do things you're not prepared to do yourself.

So, if you're a CEO, business owner, hiring manager or in HR, there is statistically a pretty good chance that you too are part of the problem.

There is no easy button for hard work.

8. To all those people getting giddy about the power of social media

If you still talk shit, people will still ignore you. They'll just ignore you in more places.

Seriously, that's all it means.

The people who are great at social media now, were great with the more traditional stuff because social media only democratises marketing for the people who already had some talent in that area.

Everyone else needs a rethink.

9. Enough with the sanctimonious bullshit

Ever since LinkedIn facilitated the uploading of images, it seems like it's getting overrun with inspirational messages posted and "liked" by what I can only assume are people desperate to create some kind of goal-post for their sad, empty, pot noodle-eating lives.

Many of them seem to fetishise rich people like Richard Branson or Warren Buffet.

Which is ironic because I'll bet you a pound to a bucket of pigshit that neither of those two ever sat around sharing hollow mantras and patting themselves on the back.

Nobody is ever going to be inspired by your motivational caption that's been overlaid on a picture of a cute kitten and an adorable puppy both trying to climb into the same slipper.

Nobody except another idiot.

Do you think life is that easy? That people's problems can be resolved by a quote urging them to "dream big" or to "go for it!"

Those idiots are all theory and no application.

10. How to decide which recruiters are worth engaging with

Job boards have become very popular over the past 10 years or so, but like most things that achieve critical mass, with that comes a very discernible drop in quality.

Most notably, the quality of the advertising (the copy, the duplications, etc..) and the quality of the candidates (unqualified, too active, no visa, etc...)

However, in this article I'd like to explore the quality of the recruiter through the eyes of a prospective candidate.

Whilst there are many recruiters who complain that the quality of candidates has declined in recent years, there are probably many more candidates that would level that same accusation at recruiters.

The most common accusation candidates level at recruiters is that they receive lots of calls, but then get very little follow-up. They're also often accused of not knowing very much about the hiring company – and that's assuming they will even disclose the hiring company's identity, which most don't.

So how can you, the candidate, wrestle back control from these recruiters who waste your time?

First, you have to understand who they are.

There are fundamentally four types of recruiter that might call you after seeing your profile on a job board or on LinkedIn. I'll rank them in order of how seriously you should take them:

1. Inhouse Recruiters

2. Agency Recruiters who own the vacancy they want to talk to you about

3. Agency Recruiters who don't own the vacancy

4. Agency Recruiters who are idiots

Let's take a closer look:

1) Inhouse Recruiters

There are two things that elevate these kinds of recruiters over the others. They're calling you about a job they *have to* fill and they're calling you from a company that they should know quite a lot about.

All calls from these types of recruiters should be entertained. If you're unsure if they're Inhouse Recruiters when they call – just ask them. One word of caution though. Some of the people calling themselves Inhouse Recruiters will, in reality, be little more than Recruitment Administrators, which will impact their understanding of the job they're calling you about.

2) Agency Recruiters who own the vacancy they want to talk to you about

These recruiters are rare, but they do exist and they tend to be pretty good at their job – given that they're capable of convincing the hiring company to only use them.

They're nearly always niche specialists and can tell you the name of their client – if not straight away then on the 2nd contact and/or on formal receipt of your CV or an email formally expressing interest.

Before engaging in any conversation, ask them if they are working on the vacancy exclusively. If they say they are, check them out by asking questions about the hiring company – ideally questions on things they're unable to get from the hiring company's website.

If they sound fluent, commit to the conversation.

3) Agency Recruiters who don't own the vacancy

These are the vast majority.

Spotting these can get a little tricky as some of them will be quite good, but the majority will just be number-crunchers.

The better ones will sound credible when you ask them about the hiring company – mostly by regurgitating text from the company's website. You may also want to ask them how long they've been recruiting and what they specialise in.

Many will try to bluff you.

Here's a phone conversation I once had with a recruiter who had seen my profile on a job board a few years back:

Agency Recruiter: "Hi Mitch, I'm calling from ABC and I'm recruiting for a role that I think you'd be suitable for and I'd just like to find out a little more about your situation?"

Me: "OK. First can I ask if you've been retained on this vacancy?"

Agency Recruiter: "What do you mean?" (I think they were buying time here)

Me: "What I'm trying to find out is if you're the only recruiter working on this vacancy or are there others?"

Agency Recruiter: "What difference does that make?"

Me: "It makes a lot of difference. If you're the only one, you're likely to have done more research before calling me and know a lot about the company, which means I won't have to waste my time talking to a recruiter who has minimal commitment from the hiring company."

Agency Recruiter: "But I do know a lot about the company."

Me: "OK, I'll ask you two questions which you have to answer. Once you do, I'll tell you whatever it is you need to know about me. Deal?"

Agency Recruiter: "OK."

Me: "First question is: What problems are the company having that this person would need to solve? Second question is: Are you the only recruiter working on this vacancy?"

Agency Recruiter: "The company aren't having any problems. And no, I'm not."

Me: "Thanks. I know I'm not going to be interested in this job."

Agency Recruiter: "How do you know that?!"

Me: "Because only the most boring jobs don't have problems that need fixing and I'm guessing this job probably isn't boring, but that you don't know much about the company, the job or the culture. Which brings me to your 2nd answer..."

Agency Recruiter: * click *

My point being, if the recruiter doesn't know much about the job, company and culture, then despite your potential suitability for that job, statistically the chances of that recruiter securing you an interview is probably less than 5%.

That will be primarily because they don't have much of a relationship with the hiring company and/or that same company has given them a very narrow brief (you know, the one that talks about the almost mythical "ideal candidate") because it's only this rarity they're prepared to pay a fee for.

4) Agency Recruiters who are idiots

These recruiters you can spot, then ignore, if they:

1. Insist on asking you questions about your experience before telling you anything about the hiring company.

2. Ask you anything that is made abundantly clear on your LinkedIn profile.

3. Call you "mate".

4. Ask what other companies you're interviewing at.

The only vacancy going on with these types of recruiters is between their ears.

It's worth taking the time to put recruiters through their paces before deciding to trust them with your candidature. This is especially true if you're looking for a better job than the one you're currently in.

If you need another job because you're unemployed or trapped in a job you hate, then you may not have the luxury of turning away recruiters – even those who are statistically most likely to waste your time.

Either way, sometimes even a cursory examination of a recruiter's credentials upfront, can save a lot of pain later.

If you're currently job hunting, you have my sympathy. I've been there and it's horrible.

11. What's the most difficult interview question?

There are lots of blogs that attempt to prepare people for that most arduous of conversations – the job interview.

Whether it's well-meaning advice on how to answer questions like "How many golf balls can you fit into a bus?" or "What are your three greatest weaknesses?", most of it is aimed at the interviewee rather than the interviewer.

I guess we all have our own ideas of what constitutes a difficult interview question, so rather than examine them all, let me be brief and give you two that I think are the most difficult to answer.

For me the most difficult question I could ever be asked in a job interview, be it face to face or over the phone, is this: "Why do you want to work here?"

I find this almost impossibly difficult to answer, mostly because it's nearly always asked far too early in the process rather than at the best time; which invariably is a day or two before a possible job offer.

It puts too much early pressure on the candidate, because the candidate almost always doesn't have enough information to answer the question. At least something that isn't a bit formulaic and bullshitty.

That's what an interview process is partly about – for the candidate to collect more information about the company/job/hiring manager so they can determine to what extent they do actually want to work there.

OK, so that's the most difficult interview question out of the way; let me leave you with what I think is the 2nd most difficult interview question.

This question needs to be asked, by the candidate, immediately after being asked why they want to work there: "I don't know why I want to work here, why don't you tell me?"

One note of caution. This question tends not to work if you're someone who needs another job (as opposed to someone who wants a better job) and/or are unemployed.

If you need another job then you're probably going to have to answer the original question with something formulaic and bullshitty.

12. What does a Purple Squirrel look like?

In case you don't know, here's a reasonable definition of the term "Purple Squirrel", according to urbandictionary.com:

"For all practical purposes, there is no such thing as a 'Purple Squirrel'; not in nature and not in the job market. It is a metaphor used by recruiters to identify the unrealistic expectations of a client company. The happy exception is when a perfect candidate, with exactly the right qualifications and experience, is found for a job opening. That person would then be referred to as a 'Purple Squirrel'."

But what does it mean to the Hiring Manager?

Firstly, no Hiring Manager uses Purple Squirrel. The term they're more familiar with is "The Ideal Candidate".

Both the Purple Squirrel and the Ideal Candidate are people whose experience is perfectly aligned with that of the hiring company. In short, they are doing the same job as the one you and/or the Hiring Manager are trying to fill.

What that translates to in real-world, practical terms, is a candidate who doesn't need to be assessed, trained or managed.

The Ideal Candidate and the Purple Squirrel are often the result of a Hiring Manager or HR person who hasn't put any thought into what they really need.

The next time you're speaking to a Hiring Manager about a job they need to fill and use the term "The Ideal Candidate", ask them to explain why they think someone would want to leave their current job (which they're doing successfully) to move to their company to do the exact same thing.

Next person to speak loses.

PART 2

Hiring Companies

13. Choosing the right recruitment supplier

A few weeks back I was reading an agency website that claimed they were better than their competitors because they "cut through the noise" and can attract better quality candidates.

Then the acid test.

I read their job ads.

All of them a list of demands ("you will be doing...", "you must have...") rounded off with a message saying that only successful candidates will be contacted.

A classic example of leakage.

Leakage can be defined as an occurrence in which secret information becomes known. In this case, that secret information is the fact that the agency doesn't know how to attract candidates to job openings.

The words are doing one thing and the actions the complete opposite.

Choosing a recruitment agency for most hiring managers is a task they take to with the same enthusiasm the rest of us have when calling Vodafone's customer service.

Some take refuge in agency claims to be specialists in whatever job it is they need to fill.

Because that is what they want to hear.

That this specialist recruiter is going to know what to do.

Because most hiring managers hate dealing with anything recruitment related.

But is someone calling themselves a specialist enough? Everyone's a specialist these days, thanks to LinkedIn.

But on closer examination, some aren't. Some of these specialists were selling mobile phones or gym memberships less than a year ago.

Despite that, selecting a recruiter based purely on age or experience can sometimes be a little short-sighted.

Probably a better way to assess a recruiter's ability to do their job well is to check their job adverts.

If their job adverts are useless, chances are they're still going to be useless when speaking to potential candidates.

Here's a checklist of what useless job adverts look like:

1. A list of "must haves" and very little about what's in it for the reader. Please note, they're not candidates yet.

2. A simple cut and paste of a job description.

3. Formulaic. Check the agency's other job ads. If they all read the same, they're formulaic.

4. Grammar and spelling. I'm talking serious stuff like "manor" instead of "manner". "Loose" instead of "lose". "Shit Manager" instead of "Shift Manager". That kind of thing.

5. Basically, jobs ads that read like the company are doing you a favour just by letting you know they have a vacancy.

The most reliable way of assessing recruiters I don't know or haven't worked with before is to see if they can produce job content that's been written freehand, with no spelling errors.

If nothing else, it shows that they at least try to interpret what their clients are looking for. And if they do that, it's evidence that some thinking has happened at some point. Thinking is good.

Checking a recruiter's social media output, especially their job ads, has got to be the most logical starting point for any Hiring Manager when deciding which recruiters to assign to their vacancies.

Many of them do this for candidates, so why not do it for recruitment suppliers too?

In fact, it's probably the closest you can get to testing a recruiter's ability in the real world.

You know, that world that's different to the one where suppliers tell you how brilliant they are.

14. Honest labour

When it comes to choosing their next job, I think there's one thing above all else that matters to most people.

And that one thing is the work.

What does the job entail doing? Who with? What are the challenges? What needs to be improved? Who else is impacted when the job is done well? What will they learn?

These are the things that people care about when they look for a job and so ought to be the drivers of recruitment adverts.

Not the company's self-proclaimed opinion of itself.

Not the funky hot-desking office environment.

And not the host of other incidental hygiene-factors that drive most attempts at creative recruitment communications that I see.

Recruitment ads that are often little more than half-baked derivations of "We're a really awesome place to work!"

If a company talks about each of their vacancies enthusiastically and honestly (and I appreciate that those two adverbs aren't natural bedfellows) and fills them with people for whom the job represents some kind of logical career evolution, then pretty much everything else would probably fall into place.

Because it's only ever really about the work.

If that's boring, unfulfilling or just plain unpleasant, no amount of ergonomic office furniture, Friday afternoons in the pub or even the stature of the company is going to make the job enjoyable – at least not in the long-term. Think Amazon, if the recent publicity about their work practices are to be believed.

So, if we accept that people care most about what they'd be doing more than who they'd be doing it for, how do we produce recruitment communications that are more likely to get the right types of response?

Here are my suggestions:

1. Be realistic about what those jobs are. What's good and what's not so good about them. Don't be afraid to reveal the not so good. It could save you a lot of time later. And it will add some credence to the good stuff.

2. Put some effort into how and where you broadcast them. Use a copywriter. Or a recruiter who knows how to use copywriters.

3. Fill them with people who can and want to do those jobs, for the right reasons.

Get those 3 things right and I reckon you've got yourself the basis of a recruitment model that can make the business sustainable, serve its customers well, grow and make money.

That's assuming the people running that business aren't

sociopaths who think they're doing the world a favour just by having job vacancies.

Start pitching your jobs in the right way to the right people. And the right people are usually those people who *can* do the job and have valid reasons for *wanting* to do the job.

Usually, the biggest reason people want to do another job is because it's more of a challenge than the one they're doing now.

Recruitment isn't rocket science.

Unless you're hiring for NASA. Then it is rocket science.

15. Aim low

Practically every single company I've ever seen cited by all the social media/employer branding experts as a model in recruitment excellence has been a massive multinational with an almost omnipresent consumer brand.

Are you going to pick up any useful scraps from the big boy's table about how you can recruit better from reading any of these citations?

No chance.

You're not going to learn anything because these companies have one massive inbuilt advantage that your company probably doesn't have – and that's thousands of candidates that already think they want to work for them.

Forget all the stuff about how they've built a state-of-the-art careers portal, made numerous videos showing what a fun and wacky place it is to work at and generated 28 billion likes on their Facebook page. That's just elaborate, corporate masturbation.

What makes the real difference is when their recruitment reps start contacting candidates.

Then their conversion ratios are very different because they're more in buying than selling mode.

They're in buying mode because candidates are far more amenable to that unexpected phone call at work and are easier to negotiate with because of the brand name.

If you're going to learn anything meaningful from how another business recruits, learn it from some company whose name isn't Apple or Starbucks.

Ask your local employer branding guru for a case study. Then wait.

16. I've got your talent right here

Sometimes I think the one big safety-pin that's holding the 3rd party recruitment industry together is the widely-held belief that the best candidates (aka "talent") are currently doing the same job for a similar company.

Let's be honest here – what's attractive about candidates already doing the same job somewhere else is that they're seen as potential employees who won't really need to be assessed, trained or managed.

They sometimes go by the term "passive candidates".

Hiring someone who doesn't need to be assessed, trained or managed seems to have become the holy grail for many risk averse managers. And if recruitment agencies have one skill, it's knowing how to feed the insecurities of their target market.

Whenever a candidate is described as "talent", invariably one of the people involved in that conversation is a hiring manager. The other is an agency recruiter.

If the hiring manager is working for a large corporate and they aren't lazy or naive, then the chances are they've become imbued with a disease that inflicts all very large businesses eventually.

That disease is called institutional arrogance.

Institutional arrogance manifests itself when a hiring manager believes that they don't have to sell their employment opportunities. That just by having a job vacancy, they're doing the world a favour.

Agency recruiters buy into this because they think the job will be easy to sell – like in this completely made-up phone exchange:

Recruiter: "Hi, I have a role I think you'll be interested in at Starbucks."

Candidate: "Why do you think I'll be interested in it?"

Recruiter: "Because it's with Starbucks."

For some reason, a lot of people involved in hiring seem incapable of putting themselves in the prospective candidate's shoes. You just need to look at 90% of job ads for evidence of this.

The kinds of hiring managers and HR folk who, when asked why someone would quit their job and work for them, take on the facial expression of a dog that's just been shown a card trick.

They struggle to see that genuinely talented people don't often look to make a sideways move into a company they don't know, unless the money on offer is obscenely high, their current employer is in some kind of trouble or the new employer genuinely offers better learning opportunities.

The primary exception is when someone has been made, or is under the threat of, redundancy. Then, all that person wants to do is maintain their lifestyle by getting another job as similar to the last one as possible.

However, recruiters have a tendency to think that anyone who's been made redundant is somehow inferior to someone who's in a job. That them being made redundant is somehow a reflection of their ability, which as we all know deep down, often isn't true.

The world is littered with "star performers" at one company who become at best average performers at their next company.

Or, candidates who act like James Bond at the interview and Mr Bean when they start work.

In my experience, the people that do tend to become star performers are those for whom the new job represents some kind of logical career progression – or a change of direction.

These people tend to work harder because they've got something to prove.

And, believe it or not, people who work harder have a habit of becoming star performers. I know, go figure.

But, the problem with these types of candidates is they're tougher to source because they're often doing different jobs with different job titles.

If companies ever stop believing the bullshit that "talent" is defined as someone already currently doing the same job, then the 3rd party recruitment industry would have to have a serious rethink about the kind of "talent" they themselves employ to work for them.

Because then, recruiters would have to start getting good at candidate assessment and less good at keyword bombing.

And that would be one long hard road for some – especially those who have yet to work out who they are, let alone who anyone else is.

So, there we have it.

Talent.

A word more abused than a Mexican at a Trump rally.

17. Employee Engagement – How far is too far?

There are few people who think having an engaged and motivated workforce isn't a good thing.

The problem is the concept is relatively new and, with the exception of a few disruptive tech companies who have sandpits in their canteens and a pool table in the boardroom, most businesses have been around long enough to remember the days when all they had to do to engage with their employees was pay them on time.

Today, those same companies look at Employee Engagement in the same way a bloke in his 40s looks at a teenager who wears his trousers halfway down his arse.

These are often the same companies that used to hire managers who could actually manage people – thus largely negating the need to bring in Employee Engagement Consultants to sprinkle the business with smiley face stickers and urge the company to hire a failed hippie to be their "Head of People Care" on about 100K a year.

Am I being too simplistic by thinking that a lot of employee engagement issues could be resolved by companies training their managers how to become better people-managers?

Maybe.

But anecdotally, I've met more people who have cited great managers as being a major influence on their career than have waxed lyrical about ergonomic office furniture or team away-days.

The whole managing people versus employee engagement issue reminds me of an exchange that allegedly happened during the making of the film *Marathon Man*, between its two main actors, Laurence Olivier and Dustin Hoffman.

If you've seen the film, you'll know that memorable scene where the on-the-run Nazi turned dentist (played by Olivier) tortures the history student (played by Hoffman) by drilling into his teeth without anaesthetic.

To play that scene, Hoffman felt he needed to look and feel very rough.

So, he put himself through a lot of personal discomfort by not eating for a day, staying up all night and not changing his clothes or showering. He may well have punched himself in the face a few times too.

When a dishevelled and tortured-looking Hoffman turned up on the set to start filming, Olivier took one look at him and said: "My dear chap, why don't you just try acting?"

There are some companies that have fully embraced the idea that Employee Engagement is actually a thing. So much so, that in the case of online retailer Zappos, they have taken to naming their employees "Zapponians".

So, not only do they sell shoes, they're also one big happy family that have wild and wacky campouts and barbecues. Is this an American thing perhaps?

I'm not knocking Zappos for attempting to make their customer service more effective (which clearly seems to be happening) or for them trying to make work more fun. I just think herding all your employees under one collective noun sounds a little cultish*.

Couldn't we all just try being better managers?

* Not a typo.

18. Bullshit 101 – "People are our greatest asset."

The "people are our greatest asset" line has got to be one of the great modern-day corporate lies.

I suspect most companies spend more money, and invest more time, in installing office printers than they do in hiring someone with specialist skills.

So why the big disconnect with what companies say and what they do?

I think what sits at its root is that most people hate the process of finding, attracting, assessing and rejecting people for jobs.

Doing it properly just isn't a lot of fun, for the most part. The most fun part is getting paid when it's finished – and that's a payoff only those in the 3rd party agency sector get to enjoy.

So, people cut corners – which is quite a normal reaction when faced with doing something you don't like.

Technology has made it easier for HR and hiring managers to hide behind automation (whilst perversely using the same automation to attract larger number of job applications) and for agencies to sell the lie that the best talent are people doing exactly the same job for a similar company.

So, whilst they're generating more candidates from channels that are cheap to use, they're also trying to reduce the amount of human interaction during the process and limit the types of candidates that are qualified to apply.

If a company really did believe the mantra that "people are our greatest asset", the department with the biggest operating budget would be HR and/or Recruitment.

But it isn't.

For many it's probably the smallest.

In many ways, as a supplier, recruitment should be one of the easiest services to sell because it causes so many companies so much discomfort.

So maybe part of the problem is that too many HR people and hiring managers are looking for an easy button and agencies, flat-fee recruiters and software companies are too prepared to sell them one.

Filling jobs is stressful and often thankless work. Maybe if we all admitted this, then maybe we could all start concentrating on tackling the work with a little more integrity?

God only knows where Big Data is going to take this jamboree of bullshit next.

19. The problem with Talent Communities

What do these 3 things have in common?

1. The Sony Betamax
2. The DeLorean car
3. Talent Communities

Answer: They all sound great in theory.

Which of these 3 things is the odd one out?

1. The Sony Betamax
2. The DeLorean car
3. Talent Communities

Answer: Talent Communities. The other 2 actually existed.

I like the theory of Talent Communities, which for the uninformed is described on Wikipedia as: "A network of candidates, employees, alumni, and social and professional networks allowing productive two-way communication between all permitting and willing connections"

The theory being that a place is created where a company can engage with people who are not employees with a view to maybe one day hiring a small number of them.

If only candidates were that compliant. Or had the time. Or really cared so much about your company that they would login to your website several times a year to chat.

As I said, I don't disagree with the theory of Talent Communities – just with what happens in the real world, where the real people live.

I think most recruiters, be they internal or agency, are under too many immediate pressures to ever be good at or have any time to spend farming large groups of candidates.

If there is one type of recruiter that *should* be good at farming candidates for future hiring, it's those very niche specialists who will always have more than one option for any one candidate.

And I doubt they're so arrogant as to herd them all over to a website to communicate with them. I suspect they use the phone regularly.

But the main problems lie with the candidates. Sorry, *potential* candidates.

I think many of those people that do bother to engage with a potential employer will stop engaging once they've had an unsuccessful interview. That puts a lot of pressure on choosing the right ones to meet.

Then there's the issue of whether candidates doing the same job for another employer are in fact the best candidates. Again, in reality, this is not true the majority of the time.

In fact, are potential candidates employed at a competitor going to even bother signing up to a Talent Community?

And if they did, wouldn't it be possible that their motives weren't that of someone looking for another job? That maybe they'd be there for entirely different reasons?

Talent Communities.

They're not communities and they're probably not talented.

20. The anatomy of a recruitment advert

Judging by all the job ads and status updates we see, it would be easy to assume that recruiters, HR and hiring managers have no basic understanding of human nature – which would be surprising given that the first two groups work in a people-centric job discipline.

More generously, maybe they just don't understand how a free-market economy works?

Free-market economies and humans are driven by personal self-interest.

Adam Smith, he of The Adam Smith Institute – Britain's leading free market neo-liberal think tank – described self-interest and business competition as the "invisible hand" that guides the economy.

In other words, if you want people to buy your stuff, you need to appeal to their self-interests.

That's fundamentally what sales is.

And what a free market economy is, is lots and lots of businesses all trying to sell their stuff.

Now let's transpose this thinking to the world of recruitment, where there are lots and lots of job vacancies that all need to attract suitable candidates. Logically, you'd think the more business-critical of those jobs would need to appeal to the self-interests of their target candidate audience, right?

Next time you look at a job ad, what you'll see at least 90% of the time, is something that follows this basic template:

1st Paragraph: Lots of rhetoric about how they are a really big / successful / dominant / nice / global / revolutionary company and why they think they're really awesome. Much of it peppered with words like "dynamic", "market leading", "unrivalled" and "growth".

2nd Paragraph: A body of text or listed bullet-points that detail some of the tasks the job involves. Sometimes they sneak in a few sentences about some of the personal qualities "the successful candidate" must have to be able to do the job.

3rd Paragraph: Next we have a number of sentences about what the candidate must bring in terms of experience, knowledge and characteristics to qualify. The experience/knowledge required is often impossibly narrow. Favourite words in this section are "ambitious", "passionate" and "hard-working".

4th Paragraph: Here they try to explain what's on offer to the candidate – sorry, the prospective candidate. Most just cite salary, hygiene factors (things like childcare vouchers and nice offices) and how the prospective candidate will find the work rewarding, on account of how awesome the hiring company thinks they are. Some will even try to squeeze in a few more demands disguised as benefits, like: "You will have many opportunities to demonstrate your talent and drive." By the way, that last sentence was taken from a real job ad – just in case you think I make this shit up.

Some will sign off their job ads with a sentence explaining that because they're really busy being awesome, they will only respond to those applicants they're interested in. Which is basically a big "fuck you" from them to their target audience.

Are these recruiters, HR people and hiring managers using the concept of self-interest to help them fill their jobs?

Yes, they are.

Their self-interests.

When it comes to doing business in general and selling in particular, the recruitment industry is living in an alternate reality.

A kind of Bizarro World.

The kind of world where the opposite of what seems right and logical appears to be the norm.

21. The "War for Talent" is dumbing everyone down

The recession is over and everyone is confident.

Companies are hiring and recruiters everywhere are happy – especially agency recruiters.

Recruiters are trumpeting how well the industry is doing, whilst conveniently forgetting that a huge chunk (91% to be exact) of its reported near £30 billion UK turnover comes from the temp/contract market where the margins are far lower than in permanent recruitment.

The "War for Talent" is back on.

So, big shortages of talent, everyone fishing in the same shallow candidate pools and recruitment agencies writing blogs and LinkedIn articles on why it's critical that companies don't waste any time making job offers to their candidates, because they won't be on the market for long.

In other words, we're back to a market that's less about recruitment and more about candidate trading.

Now we're back to agencies pitching candidates with same job/sector experience.

Now we're back to hiring managers being too lazy and/or overworked to stop and wonder why someone doing the same job for another company would be interested in working for them, especially as he didn't remember giving the recruitment agencies anything remotely resembling a brief, unless that 6-year-old job spec they emailed over counts as a brief.

Many hiring managers, HR people and internal recruiters don't know how to articulate what they really want from agencies, largely because they don't think they're going to get it even if they did ask.

This lack of confidence in the 3rd party recruitment sector has been underscored by years of agencies over-promising and under-delivering ("We have great candidates", "We're experts in your sector", "We're not like all those other agencies" etc.) and so are resigned to having to deal with multiple agencies in the hope that one of them will get lucky.

So, what is this near-mythical "recruitment consultancy service" that most of them would want if it was on offer?

In simple terms, they want an external recruitment supplier who can take a detailed brief, having already done a lot of prior research. Part of this process will involve asking difficult questions like:

"Why would someone want to leave their job and work for you?"

"Why is the average length of stay of your salespeople less than 14 months?"

"Do you think how you usually recruit new staff has influenced this high turnover?"

They then want the agency to be able to translate all that

information, insight, negatives and positives into a compelling message (or series of messages) that sell the job to the right types of potential candidates, whilst dissuading those who wouldn't be suitable.

And finally they want the agency to use this information and insight to assess candidates' suitability and personalise aspects of the sales messages to reinforce their potential interest in the job.

Ideally, they'd like one recruitment supplier to do this – partly because they don't enjoy dealing with lots of recruiters at the same time and partly because they'll easily understand why having 4 agencies all doing this would do more harm than good. Think litigious bun-fights over candidate duplication issues with the better candidates rolling their eyes and walking away.

The downside to the above scenario is that it requires the recruitment agency to be good at one crucial thing. And that one crucial thing is Recruitment.

That requires some knowledge and a lot of effort, so instead, most agencies prefer to go down the "candidate trading" route because it's what they know.

I think this is another of those vicious circles that most people can see but very few ever do anything about.

I recently stepped in at the last minute to join a webinar on the role sales plays in recruitment.

My exasperation that the participants couldn't even define what selling is, led me to describe agency recruitment as "a clusterfuck". Me not being invited back to any more of those discussions doesn't make my description of how agencies and hiring companies do business together any less true. A clusterfuck is precisely what it is.

If you're offended by bad language, please don't read that last paragraph.

22. The unpredictability of selection

I'm going to try to get through this blog entry without a) being long-winded and b) swearing.

One of the things about recruitment that can make it so compelling is its unpredictability. This is especially true for younger agency recruiters – but this unpredictability tends to become less attractive the older and smarter they get.

It doesn't matter how good you get at recruiting – there are just so many variables (i.e. human beings) that when things sometimes (and inevitably) don't go as planned, your work falls apart and you're made to look stupid.

This is particularly relevant for internal and retained recruiters, who have more access to these variables and, theoretically at least, are better placed to control them.

Things going wrong sometimes happens to even the best recruitment practitioners and is just the nature of hiring. There are just so many moving parts.

One of those moving parts are Hiring Managers and/or Company Directors.

These types of people generally hate having to find new staff. The part many seem to hate the most is meeting candidates.

I only work with SMEs and start-ups and many of these Hiring Managers/Directors tend to be "High-D" types.

High-D types are characterised by being very highly driven, goal orientated and quite impatient. They tend to prefer brief summations rather than detailed explanations and don't always have great people skills.

Spending hours sitting across a desk from potential new employees listening to them talk about their lives/jobs/careers is about as appealing to the High-D as a homophobe sitting through an Alan Carr show.

In short, they dislike interviewing and avoid doing them whenever possible.

It's one of the reasons why many of them are more likely to be suggestible to the agency recruiter who calls them with *"a hot candidate"*. They tend to buy in to anything that will mean they don't have to spend time in the recruitment process.

And so, most Hiring Managers and Company Directors tend to do one of two things.

They either hire the first half-decent person they meet and hope they turn out to be OK.

Or they just keep turning away CVs because they're holding out for that mythical perfect candidate and end up interviewing hardly anyone.

The end result being that they hire a lemon and then blame the recruiter.

Or their job goes unfilled for about 6 months.

Whichever way you look at it, it's a fucking nightmare.

I lied about the "no swearing" thing.

Sorry.

23. Staff retention is in a good place

I think the biggest single contributor to staff retention has to be the current recruitment system.

And by recruitment system, I mean things like job boards, email job alerts, job ads, LinkedIn and Applicant Tracking Systems.

I also mean things like specialist software recruiters who 4 months ago were selling cosmetics from a department store, HR people who hide behind PSLs and line managers who hate interviewing and think they're doing you a favour just by having a job vacancy.

Candidates (sorry, *potential* candidates) must sometimes take a cursory look at the jobs market and say to themselves "Yeah, I don't think so. Maybe I'll just stay where I am."

The recruitment system. Keeping people in jobs they hate like never before.

PART 3

Hiring Companies

24. Brand this

I love it when recruitment people talk about wanting to build or develop "a brand" for their agency.

I don't really love it. It drives me fucking insane.

I don't think recruiters (or worse, recruitment marketers) know what "brand" means. I didn't either, so I looked it up.

Here's what Seth Godin thinks "brand" means:

"A brand is the set of expectations, memories, stories and relationships that, taken together, account for a consumer's decision to choose one product or service over another. If the consumer (whether it's a business, a buyer, a voter or a donor) doesn't pay a premium, make a selection or spread the word, then no brand value exists for that consumer."

To put that into recruitment parlance, agencies like Hays, Michael Page and Robert Half would get clients to work with them, above all other agencies, and pay them more, simply because of their name and reputation.

As you can see, we're in polishing a turd territory here.

So, if we're comfortable with the notion that the big agencies don't have more talented recruiters per capita than the boutique agencies – and that, in all probability, the opposite is true – then it's probably safe to say that no agency has a brand.

At least not by any modern definition of the word.

Many a recruitment agency director will say that job advertising is only a part of their overall marketing spend. The bulk of that spend is reserved for things like website, content marketing, blogging, logo design, pictorial job ads and networking events.

The reality is that job advertising should be *the only* part of a recruitment agency's marketing spend – until they get that part right.

Because if your marketing is telling people you are experts in talent acquisition and your job ads demonstrably aren't acquiring any talent, then you're in a bit of trouble, credibility-wise.

Advertising, for the vast majority of job disciplines, is the most cost-effective method of reaching large numbers of potential candidates quickly.

It's also the place where the brand bullshit stops and measurable marketing starts.

As a postscript, back in the early 90s, Michael Page built their name and reputation by publishing lots of high quality job ads. No brand marketing, just attractive, well-written display ads in places like the *Daily Telegraph* and *The Grocer*. And that shit wasn't cheap back then.

25. Are relationships really that important?

I hear a lot of recruiters talk about how important relationships are – especially client relationships.

When I ask them what this means in practical/behavioural terms, most only talk about it in vague/fuzzy terms. Reading between the lines, most seem to think it's demonstrated by:

1. The client being friendly whenever they speak with them.

2. Always getting access to their vacancies – along with 5 or 6 other recruiters.

But are either of these things going to help you close more candidates?

No.

No hiring manger ever made an offer to a candidate just because they liked the recruiter.

If this is how you define a successful client relationship, they're in control, not you.

You're just gleefully running around filling about 20-25% of that client's jobs and by doing so, reinforcing the belief in their mind that your service is somewhat ad-hoc and difficult to predict.

Most meaningful business relationships are forged out of a process where a supplier is given work which they generally always deliver on. That's how a supplier is able to engender respect from the client.

If an agency recruiter can't propose an actual recruitment service they can deliver on every single time, then they're doomed to never going anywhere other than in a circular direction.

Clients don't like recruiters; partly because they don't like having to fill jobs. That's why there are so many recruitment agencies – it's not because they provide a great service, it's because everyone else hates doing recruitment.

If you're new to recruitment and wish you'd read that last sentence before accepting the job offer – I'm sorry.

What I'm saying is that it's going to be a long time before clients liking recruiters ever becomes a thing.

But they will respect recruiters who do what they say they're going to do.

Think about it. You can't like someone without first respecting them.

The only way I know of to make a recruiter/client relationship real is to offer a service where you're the only recruiter they talk to.

That way, you'll also be offering that client relief from the pain of having to pretend to like recruiters.

Free mouse-pads, buying lunches, being a nice person – all of it a hamster wheel of pointlessness if you're not able to show your best work because you're always working on the same vacancies as 4 or 5 other agencies.

Do you still think your clients do business with you because they like you? Are you looking for a way of testing your relationship with one of them?

Leave them a voicemail when they don't have any jobs to fill and see if they call you back.

26. Not all jobs sell themselves

Here's an informal (and I hasten to add, convivial) conversation I once had in a pub with the owner of a recruitment agency:

Me: "What are you in the business of selling? You know, when you break it all down."

Agency Owner: "Talent."

Me: "Fuck off, seriously..."

Agency Owner: "OK, OK... Candidates."

Me: "Who pays for those candidates?"

Agency Owner: "Clients."

Me: "OK. And why do they choose you to find them these candidates?"

Agency Owner: "Because that's what we do!"

Me: "Yeah, I know. But what is it that you can do that they can't?"

Agency Owner: "We find better candidates than they can."

Me: "So you're saying that you're better at selling jobs than they are?"

Agency Owner: "Absolutely."

Me: "So why don't your ads sell jobs?"

Agency owner: "They don't?"

Me: "No they don't. They're just prosaic lists of generalities and demands."

I then pulled out my phone and went to the jobs page on their website and starting reading some of the ads out loud.

Me: "You're just publishing content that's telling people there's a job vacancy and what they'd be doing and what they must have to apply."

Agency Owner: "Yeah but, we headhunt a lot of our candidates."

Me: "And what do you say to these candidates when you call them to make them interested in your client's jobs? I'm guessing you don't read them the job ad, right?"

Agency Owner: "Well no, obviously. We tell them what's potentially great about that job or company."

Me: "So why don't you put that stuff in your job ads?"

Agency Owner: "Err…"

Me: "But you take my point that if your job ads aren't selling anything, then you're probably not attracting the best candidates, let alone talent? Which brings me back to what it is you're really selling."

Agency Owner: "Fuck off, Mitch…"

I mentally made a note that this agency owner *might* buy copywriting training from me one day.

27. The key to getting your sales emails read

Want to know how to get more of your sales emails read?

Easy.

Compliment the recipient in the opening sentence.

This should also help you decide what you need to put in the subject line.

But, to do this, you need to do some research first.

Not quite so easy.

#noeasybuttonforhardwork

28. Bigger, badder, not better

Whenever I need to use a recruitment agency, I nearly always favour working with the smaller boutique variety rather than the large national multi-branch operations.

Most of this discrimination has been formed as the result of working for, and dealing with large recruitment agencies.

In my experience, the number of capable recruiters per capita in large agencies is much lower than in the boutiques.

In general, the bigger an agency becomes, the more it becomes about metrics and revenue rather than customer satisfaction – or the only meaningful agency metric: job to placement conversion rates.

I think that the bigger a recruitment agency gets, the more their recruitment gene pool starts to become shallower than the piss-puddle of a Chihuahua with a water infection.

This may not be the most popular opinion I've ever had.

29. A quick peek into the soul of a recruitment agency

Before deciding to apply for a job at a recruitment agency, first check out whether they have an internal recruiter.

If they do, take a look at that internal recruiter's profile on LinkedIn.

If, say around 2 years ago, that internal recruiter was working in a mobile phone shop, managing a bingo hall (sorry, leisure complex) or selling gym memberships, that should tell you pretty much everything you need to know about how seriously that agency takes recruitment and the opinion they have of their staff.

If you currently work for an agency with an internal recruiter who 6 months ago worked in admin support, apply.

See what you see, not what you think you ought to see.

30. Why recruitment agencies need to become pigs

Bear with me on this one.

It must be blatantly obvious to anyone who works in the hiring business that recruitment agencies have received quite a lot of flak over the past few years – some of it caused by oafish sales tactics and some of it by their diminishing ability to deliver a viable recruitment service in the face of the burgeoning inhouse recruitment sector.

So, how did we get here?

With the advent of the Internet came a lot of predictions that it would spell the end of recruitment agencies. That didn't happen because the job boards loaded their pricing in the agencies' favour and recruitment consultants got better at using the Internet than HR people.

No surprises there.

Now that HR finally woke up to the fact that for recruitment to really work they need to bring on board their own inhouse recruitment specialists, those initial predictions are starting to look like they could at least partially come true.

So, what can a recruitment agency do to start reclaiming its relevance and its margins?

Well, that is a huge question that can vary depending on the sector it serves and the candidate types it trades in – so for the purposes of this piece, I'm going to assume that the agency-type in question is a broad vertical market specialist and places permanent candidates, but it could equally apply to any generalist agencies.

It will probably be less relevant to those agencies that specialise in niche skills that inhouse recruiters can't easily find and engage with. Yet.

Recruitment agencies have long been addicted to the thrill of what I call "the easy placement". That happens when:

- They receive a job from a company (often with minimal commitment).

- They happen to either know of a suitable candidate or find one quickly.

- Interviews happen.

- That candidate gets the job.

- An invoice is then raised for anything up to 20K.

Those kinds of rewards for doing very little work can become addictive. I know because I've been there.

You might argue that placements made this way are payback for all that other work that didn't result in a placement fee. But that's not the point. And it's definitely not the point to the company the agency made the placement with.

Thereafter, everything the recruitment agency does is

geared around collecting certain types of candidates to increase their chances of getting lucky. Much of this activity is wasted and nearly all of it is advertised on job boards.

But it only takes a couple of placements like that every month for that business model to take root. Cue more companies getting cold-called and being asked for a chance to throw a candidate or two at some of their open jobs and more candidates responding to adverts that the agency is never actually going to do any meaningful work on.

Both are (and have been for years) being set up for probable disappointment.

Which brings us to the flak recruitment agencies are getting today.

So, the old model isn't working anymore because there are a lot less HR people desperate for candidates to appease their critical and time-poor line managers and there are a hell of a lot more candidates who've grown cynical about responding to job ads that they're not even going to get a response to (let alone a shot at an interview) all because they know there's a strong likelihood the agency has little sway with the hiring company.

What are HR people, inhouse recruiters, hiring managers and SME owners more likely to need these days when they do need to use an agency? My experiences as an agency recruiter, search-business owner and contract inhouse recruiter is that these people need (and more importantly, want) commitment.

Let me say that again, loudly.

THEY WANT COMMITMENT.

If you're an agency recruiter, most companies now want you to commit to filling a particular job, regardless of the salary level. Just like companies who have an inhouse recruitment team expect those recruiters to commit to filling their jobs.

They would rather have one external recruiter that is totally committed to filling one of their open jobs than 10 of them all saying they'll "have a look around and fire over some CVs" with one of them getting lucky.

But that commitment is a two-way street.

The company also must commit. When they do, many will gladly pay some of the fee upfront – but you have to sell the benefits of why it's in their best interests to make that commitment.

When this happens, what you'll have is a real client, rather than an ad-hoc customer – which pretty much defines what a typical buyer of recruitment agency services is.

These clients will want you to take problems away from them, not add more by sending speculative CVs and pissing off their target candidate audiences. They want value for money and they want this value to be evidenced by you working hard for them.

They want you to share some of their pain because that's how real relationships are formed – both in business and socially.

So instead of asking for jobs, saying that you "have the best candidates" (which 8 times out of 10 you don't) and punting out a few CVs of candidates you've not met, why not try actually selling something for a change?

Don't sell them the line that you're not actually selling them anything (which is what contingency recruiting basically is) – sell them on the fact that you will not stop working until you fill their job.

Then sell them on the fact that you will work to a pre-agreed sourcing strategy.

Sell them on the fact that you'll produce superior attraction materials to help prise out the best candidates from jobs they may no longer be enjoying.

Sell them on the fact that you'll genuinely assess who the best candidates are, manage all of them professionally and offer the client a realistic guarantee period when they hire one of them.

If you sell a real recruitment service, many companies will want to pay you upfront.

And that in turn will enable you to deliver much more and create a relationship where the client will never want to talk to a competitor agency – because you'll now be enjoying a 100% success rate rather than the 20-30% success rate you currently have.

Then once you have just a handful of these real clients, your sales-pipeline becomes more forecastable. Then management starts getting a bit happier too.

Now you're a real recruiter who solves problems from start to finish, rather than someone who trades candidates on the fringes of a hiring process you have zero control over.

Some of these jobs will be quite easy to fill too – the difference now being that you've spent real time working the pre-agreed recruitment plan and worked all of the sourcing channels so that now your client is no longer simply buying a candidate.

No, now they're buying something much more valuable; they're buying the confidence that they're probably hiring the best candidate currently available.

The client will love the fact that you've worked hard on their vacancy, rather than plucked a candidate from a database. And regardless of whether you do this or not, many companies see this as the extent of what many recruitment agencies do.

The relationship will be sealed when they don't wince when they see your bill.

Which brings us back to the "pig" thing

Recruitment can be viewed as a plate of ham and eggs. The chicken is involved, but the pig is committed.

Most recruitment agencies need to stop being the chicken.

31. Has there ever been a worse opening to a job ad than this?

"I'm currently recruiting for this position. Please click on the job title below to view the Job Description and apply to it!"

Apart from "My client, a dynamic market leader…" obviously. That one's been stinking up the Internet for years.

Where's the hook? The attention grabber? The reason why someone might click?

Is letting them know they're going to be reading a job description really going to help?

Or are they only looking for people who *need* another job rather than those who might *want* a *better* job?

Have the people posting this stuff never been potential candidates themselves?

A lot gets talked about the collective reputation of the recruitment industry – much of it justified, some of it not.

But if there's one aspect of recruitment agency behaviour that is open to critical scrutiny by everyone – and by everyone, I mean owners, directors and hiring managers of other businesses – it's their job advertisements.

One of the key ways I gain insight into a business is to see how they advertise their careers. If you know what you're looking for, there is much insight to be gleaned just by carefully reading a company's job ads. It's a window into their soul.

When you see job ads that all pretty much say the same thing and that rehash the same stock phrases and clichés, it's probably safe to say that's an organisation that has a relatively low opinion of the act of recruiting and of the people they're trying to attract.

If that organisation is a recruitment agency – an entity who by its very definition are supposed to be experts in attracting and assessing people for jobs – then it's hard to imagine why any company in its right mind would use them to find candidates.

If an agency can't sell a job in writing, how are they going to do it over the phone or in person?

When you post jobs on the Internet, everyone can see them.

And if those job ads are poor, all you're doing is slowly but surely embedding a reputation of being an agency that probably isn't very good at its claimed area of expertise.

32. Life changers

The next recruiter that tells me they love their job because "they have the power to change people's lives" is going to get introduced to the business end of my shoe.

If you're one of those recruiters that actually believes this, allow me to give you a lift back to planet Earth.

You're not a Social Worker.

You're not a Life Coach.

You're not a Career Counsellor.

You're not some Archangel of Altruism either.

You don't change people's lives. You sometimes get paid by companies to provide them with options for jobs they're trying to fill.

Some of those options attend interviews and a small number of them end up working for that company. An even smaller number end up enjoying working there.

Of those that do, *they* made that positive change happen, not you.

Did you only send that one person to the company because you unequivocally knew they were a perfect fit? No, of course you didn't.

You either built a shortlist or you spot-traded some candidates out to any number of different potential employers who might entertain the notion of hiring them.

In the same way that you're not responsible for all the people you've placed with a new employer who've gone on to hate that job. And yes, there were some of those too.

Claiming your actions have a direct correlation to people going on to lead more fulfilling lives is the same as aimlessly firing an arrow and drawing a bullseye around wherever it lands.

You're a recruiter. Your job is to make hiring easier and/or more effective for companies in exchange for money. If you're good at it, you probably make a decent living – and in some cases, it may even be more money than you deserve. Quit while you're ahead.

But please, do not try to evangelise that there's some kind of social significance to what us recruiters do – because there isn't.

If you want to really change people's lives, work at your local Job Centre or find jobs for the mentally ill, the disabled and the terminally unemployed.

Now *that* would be some real life-changing action.

33. Should recruitment agencies be bothered about "Candidate Experience"?

Depending on what statistics you read, some 55% of applicants believe the standard of recruitment practice has declined.

I'm surprised it's that low.

Creating a good candidate experience has become the latest trend in recruitment – there are even awards function dedicated to it. Or in other words, recruiters finding yet another excuse to dress up and pat themselves on the back for not pissing off as many people as their competitors.

The rationale behind creating a good candidate experience is that if candidates are treated well, they'll think more positively of the company's brand and talk about it to their friends, thus gradually making hiring easier.

But there's one thing we need to get out of the way upfront, so we can put the whole candidate experience debate into some kind of context.

Everybody dislikes being a candidate.

People find job-hunting extremely stressful and rarely ever relish the prospect of applying for jobs.

So, in a business arena like recruitment that people dislike being a part of, almost by default, how feasible is it to spend time and effort on improving something that candidates already hate?

That seems about as pointless as reading a child a bedtime story whilst *Nightmare on Elm Street* is playing full blast on the TV.

How much time and effort do you really need to invest in improving the candidate experience if you're on a hiding to nothing anyway? I'll leave that for you to decide.

But if you do feel it's important, let's explore what the problems really look like and simple ways to resolve them.

Having a hiring process that creates a good candidate experience ranges from improving everything from job ads, career sites and applicant tracking systems through to responding to all CVs received and giving meaningful feedback to those candidates that were interviewed.

The last two are the only things candidates really care about, and paradoxically, are the two things that recruiters and hiring companies are reportedly the worst at.

So, what's the answer?

That will depend on what type of recruiter you are. If you work inhouse, then your need for an improvement in this area is going to be different (and arguably more important) than those working agency side.

Let's talk a closer look at agencies.

What kind of recruiter are you?

Again, your commitment to candidate experience will vary depending on whether you're a temp agency or a perm agency.

Temp agencies are often placing the same people several times over and so managing a larger volume of applicants and all the associated admin should make their approach to this different to the perm recruiters.

It should also be noted that temp recruiters are often more able to be transparent about their client's identity and, because they may have recruited for the same client many times before, will often have a better understanding of those clients. That all contributes to them being better equipped to make the process less arduous for candidates.

Then we need to look at the different types of perm recruiters.

The generalists tend to bother less with candidate experience because their supply-chain of potential candidates is inexhaustible. This will be manifested by their constant need to find new clients because their candidate quality is usually somewhat inconsistent.

The niche specialists have an altogether different set of problems.

For them, their candidate pools are not inexhaustible and care does have to be taken to nurture positive relationships with their target candidates. They *have to* be more sensitive to their needs, if only because referrals are (or should be) a valuable source of new business.

In essence, the more niche the agency recruiter, the more critical candidate experience becomes.

Then there's the question of whether a bad candidate experience affects the agency's brand or the hiring company's brand. That's assuming they even have a brand that can be articulated – which most don't.

Problems at the front end of a recruitment process (before the recruiter reveals who the hiring company is) tend to damage the agencies reputation, and problems at the back end (after the recruiter has revealed the company and arranged interviews) tend to damage both the agency's and the hiring company's reputations.

When candidates feel aggrieved by any aspect of the recruitment process, they tend to think that if a hiring company are this bad (or choose bad agencies to represent them), then they're probably going to be bad to work for.

How a company recruits is often a window into their soul.

The bottom line is that most candidates are low-maintenance and do not have particularly high expectations when it comes to their job-hunting experience. They just need the adverts and job briefs to be accurate, the rejections prompt and the interview feedback as honest as legal compliance will allow.

If you're a recruitment agency and you want to improve the candidate experience, either for yourself or for your better clients, here's my simple 3 step plan to help you achieve this:

1. Know a lot about the job, the company, their culture and their vision. This will come from either experience of past assignments or by taking a really detailed brief and by asking some tough questions. This will then have a huge impact on the quality of candidates you're able to source and attract.

2. Produce adverts that stand out from the crowd. And make them easy to respond to.

3. Get back to all candidates when you say you'll get back to them. If you haven't given a time when you'll get back to them, get back to them anyway. This is all most candidates want.

But remember, given that most candidates hate the process of finding a new job, the most you can realistically hope for is that candidates don't also hate you.

If they don't hate you (assuming they even remembered you), chances are they'll talk to you again at some point in the future. And if people are always willing to talk to you, you're in business.

Great candidate experience isn't going to happen just by spending money on fancy websites, clever tech or building an employer brand – in fact I'd even argue that there is no such thing as a great candidate experience to anyone other than the person who ends up getting the job.

But it will happen by having great recruiters.

There are lots of differing definitions of what constitutes a great recruiter. For some it's personality based and for others it's about billing numbers.

I think the safest way to measure how good a recruiter is, is to look at the percentage of jobs they work on that they fill.

A great recruiter fills at least 80% and a weak recruiter fills around 10%. The industry average across all agency recruiters is somewhere between 20% and 25%.

Therefore, a decent candidate experience is, in all logical probability, just a by-product of a decent recruiter managing the vacancy.

34. Why recruitment agencies can't sell

You have an opportunity to talk to a new potential client. They have a job to fill and they've decided that they're going down the agency route.

A classic selling situation.

Except that it isn't for the vast majority of recruitment agencies – because they've got nothing to sell.

Most recruitment agencies default method of doing business is contingency – meaning they'll only charge a fee if they find the candidate who is hired.

Given that an agency will fill 20% or less of all the jobs they ever work on, what they're really selling is "Maybe". Or to give it its longer title "I Might Fill This Job If I Can Be Bothered To Do Any Meaningful Work, Or Get Lucky".

Any idiot can say they *might* do something – and many often do.

But what often happens in these selling situations is that the agency will use sales language to foster the notion that by giving them access to the vacancy, they have the expertise/database/knowledge to *definitely* fill that vacancy.

That's not selling. That's overselling.

Recruitment agencies can't sell because the reality is they've got nothing to sell.

Selling is where you identify a client need, present a case for solving that need, and then deliver a product or service that provides that solution. Doesn't matter if it's a piece of software or a box of lightbulbs.

Worst case scenarios of selling something that won't be delivered is basically scamming.

Now, I'm not saying that recruitment agencies are scammers because they most definitely aren't, but that gap between what's being presented and what's being delivered offers a clue as to why so many people have such little regard for agency recruiters.

Many of you will say things like "Yeah but we're not like the others, we're more professional and experts in our field" – but you are the same because you act in the same way and do business in the same way.

You cannot sell a contingency recruitment service. You can only oversell it.

35. Chickens, Pigs and Monkeys

In the previous blog, I used chickens to describe the current state of the recruitment agency landscape and pigs to describe how that state could be improved.

Now I'm going to use monkeys to describe how they got there in the first place.

The story I'm going to cite is the research study called "The 5 Monkey Experiment". You'll be able to find out more about this experiment online.

Here's a summary.

They started with a cage containing five monkeys. Inside the cage, they hung a banana on a string with a set of stairs placed under it.

Before long, a monkey went to the stairs and started to climb towards the banana. As soon as he started up the stairs the psychologists sprayed all the other monkeys with ice cold water.

After a while, another monkey tried to obtain the banana. As soon as his foot touched the stairs, all the other monkeys were sprayed with ice cold water.

It wasn't long before all the other monkeys would physically prevent any monkey from climbing the stairs.

Now, the psychologists shut off the cold water, removed one monkey from the cage and replaced it with a new one. The new monkey saw the banana and started to climb the stairs.

To his surprise and horror, all the other monkeys attacked him. After another attempt and attack he discovered that if he tried to climb the stairs, he would be assaulted.

Next, they removed another of the original five monkeys and replaced it with a new one. The newcomer went to the stairs and was attacked. Even the previous newcomer took part in the punishment with enthusiasm.

Likewise, they replaced a third original monkey with a new one, then a fourth, then the fifth. Every time the newest monkey tried to climb the stairs, he was attacked.

The monkeys had no idea why they were not permitted to climb the stairs or why they were beating any monkey that tried.

After replacing all the original monkeys, none of the remaining monkeys had ever been sprayed with cold water. Nevertheless, no monkey ever again approached the stairs to try for the banana.

Why not? Because as far as they know, that's the way it's always been around here.

Running a recruitment agency on the contingency model used to make sense. But that was back in the day before the Internet, job boards, LinkedIn, social media and internal recruitment teams.

Now it makes no sense because too many people are all approaching the same much smaller groups of candidates.

But they keep doing it because that's all they know.

Old habits get ingrained and jargon, clichés and sales patter become stereotyped.

Now the only real difference is they've learned how to not fill jobs at broadband speeds.

This blog was written by a monkey who escaped from the cage 15 years ago.

36. Another quick peek into the soul of a recruitment agency

The other day I saw a Recruitment Trainer job advertised as a status-update on LinkedIn with an annual salary of £25K + 5K bonus.

When I asked if the job was part-time, the recruiter who posted the update deleted my comment.

Pretty much everything that's wrong with recruitment agencies is encapsulated right there.

Or to elaborate, recruitment agencies paying next-to-nothing to failed recruiters to train their staff to continue being the types of recruiters that drove so many companies to build their own inhouse recruitment function.

And then closing their eyes and singing "la, la, la, la la" at the tops of their voices.

37. This is kids' stuff. Anyone can do it

Today I saw a job advert for Trainee Recruitment Consultant.

What drew me to look at the ad was the pre-sell that the agency is "ranked 19th on the Recruiter Hot 100 list", whatever that is.

The ad mostly talked about how lovely their offices are, which is fine if that's what you think is going to be the most appealing aspect of the job, but it was this sentence particularly caught my eye:

"As a trainee recruitment consultant, you will be doing a full 360 recruitment role."

First of all, even experienced agency recruiters don't do a 360-degree recruitment role. Only retained external recruiters and inhouse recruiters do that. This is one of the agency world's major blind-spots – thinking that what makes a full cycle recruitment job is that they get to deal with hiring companies AND candidates.

There are a lot more angles involved in filling a job than just being sent a job spec and having a few phone screens with candidates.

There's taking a full brief, challenging the hiring manager on the unrealistic aspects of what they're looking for, working out what the sales propositions for that job/company are going to be, how to communicate those sales propositions, interviewing and assessing the right candidates and, of course, rejections and general housekeeping.

But a bigger and more pervasively damaging blind-spot is these agencies thinking that inexperienced young people with a desire to earn a lot of money are ever going to be taken seriously by clients with strategically important jobs to fill.

Letting trainees telephone potential clients to do anything other than make an appointment for an experienced recruiter to have a phone conversation seems like utter madness to me.

Correction, *is total and utter madness.*

The people who decide to let this happen are either a bit stupid or incredibly arrogant.

Trainees working as 360-degree recruiters?

There's the problem with many recruitment agencies, right there.

38. Three powerful questions that can set you apart from your competitors

Whether you like (or believe) it or not, most Hiring/HR Managers don't see a lot of difference between the various contingency recruitment agencies they deal with.

Sure, they may engage with you in a spirit of cooperation – but that is mostly down to either their supplier-management skills or their desperation in trying to fill the role they've just given you access to.

That's because nearly all recruitment agencies say and do the same things. Generally, the two factors that set recruiters apart are either:

1. Their personality.

2. Their track record in filling jobs or submitting high quality candidates to that particular company.

Now, both of those are good enough platforms from which to build a more sustainable client/supplier relationship; however, what percentage of all the companies you ever speak to do those conditions exist in?

For the majority, that number is probably less than 20%.

That leaves around 80% of all your hiring company interactions dealing with people who've rarely, if ever, spoken to you before. And those are some of the toughest conversations you'll have – once they've given you a role to try and fill.

What many of the better recruiters then do is:

1. Clarify some of the details on the job spec.

2. Ask what else they've done to fill the job and how many agencies are involved.

3. Pre-close for some interview slots.

Then they join the race to find possible candidates as quickly as possible.

Sometimes this client/recruiter conversation is the result of a cold-call where the phrase "we have great candidates" or "we are specialist in this field" has featured prominently.

This is when the "these guys pretty much all sound the same" thought kicks in to the client's brain.

OK, so what can we do to start changing the direction of that thought pattern?

Here are 3 questions that if asked (with the appropriate explanations and follow-up questions) will start to differentiate you from the other agencies. They may also help you fill more of these jobs you're being given by these indifferent hiring companies:

Q1: Who have you previously met, worked with or interviewed, that you think might be the right kind of person for this job?

Q2: What specific companies have previously successful candidates and current staff worked for, before joining you?

Q3: Would you have any objections to me speaking to members of your team to get referrals to people they may know?

The first question sets the tone for the differentiation you're trying to establish. Regardless of the answer, the person on the other end of the phone will start to take you more seriously because you're already demonstrating your ability to think laterally and your desire to help solve their problem.

The second question acts as an information gatherer (assuming you don't already know the answer) and continues to condition the Hiring Manager into thinking they may finally be talking to the right recruiter.

The third is the jackpot question – especially if they agree to the request, because once you're able to talk to existing employees on the recommendation of the Hiring Manager (I don't think many HR Managers will agree to this), not only do you have access to high quality candidate referrals, you also have access to high quality information about the job and the company.

But more than that, what you're really doing is leveraging the power of referrals, recommendations and other people's networks.

Most Hiring Managers don't do this themselves either because they're too busy, don't like doing recruitment or simply hadn't thought of it before. Whatever their reason, most will find the logic of doing it inescapable and many will be happy for someone else to both do it, and follow up on it.

Asking these questions also connects with the single most powerful and cost-effective single recruitment tool there is – The Employee Referral Scheme.

Some companies have them (around 30% if my memory is correct) and most don't work. They don't work because the companies don't ask for them – and what I mean by that is nobody in the company approaches another employee face-to-face and asks them who they might know.

Employee referrals are incredibly powerful and many companies don't leverage them properly – but that doesn't mean you shouldn't be able to.

You'd need to demonstrate your professionalism before many companies would give you official access to their employees in this way – but if they do, they're clearly saying that they trust you and have more belief in you than their other agency suppliers.

Try it. It works.

One word of caution. Don't blow it by trying to recruit any of these employees for other clients.

39. The secret to cold-calling

Ever seen those training providers that promise to help you unlock the secrets to cold-calling?

Most of the time this "secret" turns out to be something inane like sounding happy when you make the call or only doing it when the sun's shining.

What seems to drive most of the recruitment sales training I've ever seen is the fact that cold-calling is an omnipresent part of a recruiter's life – and so they had better get good at it.

Frankly, I think that's bullshit.

It's bullshit not because it isn't true, because it is. It's bullshit because it doesn't have to be true.

Cold-calling is probably the toughest part of the sales process because it's time-consuming, it's boring and repetitive and because it's often hard to even get through to the decision-maker. The only things that makes it a worthwhile activity are:

1. If what you're selling has a high-margin, one-off sale price.

2. If the cold-call is the first step in a longer sales journey where the customer can regularly buy an increasing number of products/services from you.

Recruiters can fall into either or both of those categories.

The first when they're canvassing out a specific (and available) candidate and the second when they're broadly looking for jobs to fill.

Canvassing out candidates can be a valid way of establishing some credibility with a potential client, but it requires some decent market research before any calls are made. Sadly, many recruiters don't bother doing this, preferring instead to just mailshot a CV to as many companies they think might be relevant as possible.

Assuming they're able to establish some credibility with that company, what next?

Invariably what the recruiter is looking for next is a regular source of new jobs to work on – which brings us to the 2nd category.

The trouble with getting more jobs from more companies is that on average, a recruiter only fills about 1 in 5 of the jobs they get given access to. And I'm being generous here – for some it's closer to 1 in 8.

That means that around 80% of the time the recruiter is going to disappoint the company who give them a vacancy to work on.

"But sometimes I will fill some jobs with some of those clients!" I can already hear you cry.

True.

But all you're really doing is entrenching the perception in the client's mind that your delivery is somewhat ad-hoc and difficult to predict. That every time that client gives you a vacancy, they're going to also need to give the same vacancy to 3 or 4 other agencies too.

If that's the pinnacle of how your clients see you then I have some bad news – you're always going to have to be spending large chunks of your time cold-calling. The upside is that this is good news for the recruitment and sales training industry, whose best interests are served by agencies continually needing to cold-call.

There is no secret to being good at cold-calling when all you're selling is probable disappointment. One feeds the other.

So, there's your "secret", right there.

Sorry.

40. Looking for a safe stance on the use of exclamation marks in recruitment advertising? Me neither

The exclamation mark is known informally as a bang or a shriek. It's frequently used in fiction and then mostly to express strong feeling in spoken dialogue.

There are broadly 3 types of people who use exclamations marks when writing:

- Amateurs
- Children
- Fashion Journalists

Clients don't want their recruitment agencies to be any of these things – which makes the fact that some consistently use exclamation marks in their job postings all the more surprising.

So, leaving the cheap jibes aside for a moment, why is it not a good idea to use exclamation marks in recruitment advertising?

When you run an ad with the headline *Sales Manager!* and a first line that starts *Exciting Local Company!!!* it quickly raises the enthusiasm to a level that the recruiter is going to find very hard to match when the cold hard reality of working for a struggling engineering company in Runcorn needs to be delivered later.

So, unless the advertised job really is worthy of a breathless jollity not seen since Lorraine Kelly interviewed Graham Norton on breakfast television, cut out the exclamation marks and make the candidate-management part of your job a little easier.

Then there's the most important piece in this part of the recruitment process.

The readers.

Please note, they're not candidates yet.

Naturally, you want your advert to create a good impression and for the readers to take you seriously as a business professional. That means writing something that is calm, measured and accurate.

It can still sell – it just doesn't need the shrieks at the end of the sentences.

That kind of gushy enthusiasm is off-putting at best and patronising at worse.

And it doesn't matter who your target audience is because they'll all feel like they're being oversold to or being talked down to.

And if that loses you only one qualified candidate, it isn't worth doing. You owe your clients at least that.

More broadly, it's been argued by smarter people than me, that an adult's sanity is inversely proportional to the number of exclamation marks they use when writing on the Internet. Maybe that's a subject for another day.

Stop using exclamation marks in your job adverts, or anything else you write for that matter.

If you really can't help yourself – hire a copywriter.

41. Recruitment, stripped bare

When you distil down everything a recruiter does (or should do), there are only two things they need to be good at to be effective.

Those two things are:

1. Candidate Attraction

2. Candidate Assessment

Pretty much everything else is an action that supports one of these two activities.

Research, sourcing, channel management, social media, candidate engagement, negotiating and offer management – all of them are support activities to the two critical areas of recruitment: selling jobs to the right candidates and then assessing them.

Of course, this assumes that you've taken a detailed brief, asked difficult questions and can make the hiring manager see that hiring someone who is doing exactly the same job for a competitor is, more often than not, an unsustainable approach to finding new employees.

Recruitment is, in simple terms, about finding enough of the right types of people and then assessing which ones are going to be the most likely to succeed.

So, who are the best recruiters?

I think the best recruiters are Company Directors, Hiring Managers and Internal Recruiters. Or rather, they *should* be.

These are the people that know the most about the business, possess an understanding of their culture and have the most to lose by getting it wrong. The people with skin in the game.

They're also the people least equipped to put all of that knowledge into practice.

The Directors and Hiring Managers tend to lack objectivity and have an unrealistic view of what it takes to fill a job and the Internal Recruiters are generally overworked.

All of which means that effective candidate attraction and candidate assessment is what they need, and want, from any 3rd party recruitment supplier they give a vacancy to.

They want an agency to be able to sell a job effectively, whether that be via adverts or direct approaches – and to then be capable of screening and assessing the best of those who respond.

If you're an agency recruiter and you can convince a company of your ability to do both those things, they'll work with you on your terms and keep coming back.

That's assuming you can actually do both those things of course.

Being great at sourcing isn't the same as being able to build intelligent dialogue with potential candidates once you've found them.

In the same way that pitching candidates looking for a sideways move into a similar company isn't recruiting. That's called candidate trading. Candidate trading is a form of recruitment that embeds the belief in a client's mind that agencies are only useful for accessing same-sector candidates.

The problem with having those types of clients is that they'll never really value you. That is a tough customer type to have to make a living from.

Candidate trading is a perfectly legitimate way of making a living, but please, do not kid yourself that you're a recruiter.

Trading candidates on the open market is fun – especially when you're young, but it does start to become a bit tedious as you become older, get married, have kids and take on a mortgage. Then, not knowing where your fees are coming from becomes a lot less attractive.

So, what kind of recruitment practitioner do you want to be 5 years from now?

One that is forever hitting the phones looking for companies who are lazy or stupid enough to believe that populating their businesses with candidates prepared to make sideways moves constitutes great recruitment practice?

Or one that has a portfolio of loyal clients whose hiring problems you can solve by building bespoke recruitment campaigns and delivering candidates who are a better long-term fit for their businesses?

Do you want to be a Recruitment Consultant or a Candidate Trader?

The choice is yours.

42. The marketing advice branding experts don't want recruitment agencies to hear

There's loads of marketing advice out there telling recruitment agencies to differentiate themselves. Most of it is ignored for two reasons:

1. The advice is shit.

2. The agency realises they aren't any different to any other agency and so just do what they're all doing. This is called "Me Too Marketing" and basically means the agency will just say what every other agency is saying.

You know, stuff like:

"...exceeding our clients' expectations"

"...get to know your business and your culture"

"...world class recruitment service"

"...market leading"

"...award winning"

All of it boring and much of it total horseshit.

To be fair to agencies, they do all broadly work the same way and there are only so many things you can say about their business model. All that's left are the adjectives the agency chooses to convey how great they think they are, and let's be honest here, nobody's buying that.

So, we're agreed that a recruitment agency's funnel of good marketing material is incredibly narrow, right? What can they do to widen that funnel?

There is one thing that all agencies have that would enable them to massively widen their range of marketing content.

Jobs.

Many of them different and across a range of employers or sectors.

That's an inexhaustible supply of fresh marketing material. Jobs that all have different environments, bosses, cultures, products, services, locations, benefits, financial rewards, etc.

Let me emphasis this point because it's important:

YOU WILL LITERALLY NEVER RUN OUT OF STUFF TO WRITE ABOUT!

If agencies spent less of their marketing budget on things like their website, branding, blogging, mass emailing and posting inane quotes on LinkedIn and more of it on simply producing great job advertising, they'd never run out of new things to say, all of which would help prove to the outside world that they're better recruiters than their competitors.

Can building a reputation as a recruitment agency that produces great job ads ever be anything other than a good thing?

The worst that can happen is you'll find better candidates.

The best that can happen is that candidates and clients start to call you because they've seen you consistently publish good job ads – job ads that have conditioned them to believe that you are better recruiters than those other agencies who write the same "our client, a dynamic market leader…" bullshit.

I suppose it could be argued that the agency could cheat by using copywriters instead of writing their ads themselves. For me, that wouldn't be cheating, it would be money well spent.

The reality is that copywriters are only capable of producing good job ads if they've been given a good job brief, so that wouldn't work for very long. Most copywriters I know would rather starve than have to churn out made-up copy on jobs that all sound the same.

So, stop churning out the same narrow shit as every other agency that basically reads as little more than *'We're really good at our jobs, honestly!'* and instead start crafting well-written job ads that give a live demonstration of your ability to attract the right people to your client's job vacancies.

Showing is always more powerful than telling.

43. Concerned that robots might be able to do your job? Don't be

I've seen a lot of articles on LinkedIn that talk about how Artificial Intelligence could displace the need for recruiters.

Once you've read one, you've read them all. Most are too long and basically just say that within most of our lifetimes, robots could have replaced human recruiters.

Great. Bring it on.

I'm looking forward to the day when robots will be doing our jobs. Obviously, robots don't need salaries, which means that we can muck about at home all day on full pay. That's how this robot thing is going to work, right?

Plus, these robots will probably need managing. Think about it. If you've seen *Terminator*, you'll know how real that shit can get if they're left to their own devices.

What we could end up with is these robots only giving jobs to other robots.

Then McKinsey would bring out a ground-breaking report called "The War for Robots".

And then we'd all really be in trouble.

44. What does the future for recruitment agencies look like?

Ever since the Internet came along, people have been questioning if, or how, recruitment agencies would cope with the new democratisation of candidate data the Internet ushered in.

The recruitment agency market has coped. They've coped largely through becoming more niche and most companies remaining relatively ignorant about how to hire staff.

The job boards loading their pricing in the agencies' favour also helped.

Recruitment agencies have survived, mostly without having to change how they do business.

Ever since that argument was put to bed, people now speculate whether agencies can continue to survive given their collective poor reputation.

The reality is that the immediate future for recruitment agencies looks fairly bright, if only because we're out of recession and many companies are still obsessed with hiring candidates with same sector/job title experience – an attitude that's been cultivated by the aforementioned niche recruiters.

Neither of those two states are ever going to encourage agencies to change their business model.

So, what will?

For me, that will only start happening when the numbers of inhouse recruiters moving back into the agency world escalates beyond the trickle it currently is.

And even then, the change will be slow and gradual.

And I mean genuinely skilful, intelligent inhouse recruiters rather than the glorified administrators some companies seem to think pass as recruiters.

When more of these types of inhouse recruiters start working agency side, they'll start to educate the agency how recruitment works on the other side of the fence.

They'll be able to offer insight into how those companies think, what they need and what their perception of recruitment agencies really is.

Then these recruitment agencies will become better informed as to what to sell to these companies – and how to sell it.

That will, I think, be the next evolutionary stage of the recruitment agency sector's journey towards greater professionalism and stability of revenue.

It ain't happening tomorrow though.

Made in the USA
Las Vegas, NV
19 January 2021